I0796068

Bob Feller

THE STORY OF THE CLEVELAND INDIANS

Pitcher Shane Bieber

THE STORY OF THE

CLEVELAND INDIANS

JIM WHITING

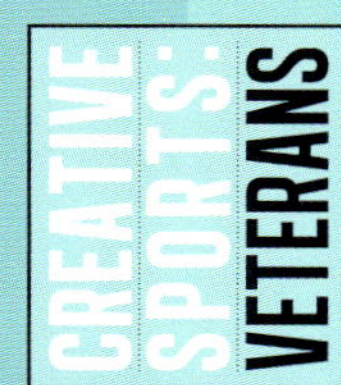

C. C. Sabathia

CREATIVE EDUCATION / CREATIVE PAPERBACKS

Published by Creative Education and Creative Paperbacks
P.O. Box 227, Mankato, Minnesota 56002
Creative Education and Creative Paperbacks are imprints of The Creative Company
www.thecreativecompany.us

Design and production by Blue Design (www.bluedes.com)
Art direction by Rita Marshall
Printed in China

Photographs by Alamy (Carlos Gonzalez/Minneapolis Star Tribune/TNS, UPI), Christie's Auction House, Getty Images (Victor Baldizon/MLB Photos, Al Bello/Allsport, Lisa Blumenfeld, Bruce Bennett Studios, Jonathan Daniel, Diamond Images, Focus on Sport, Otto Greule Jr, Harry How, Paul Jasienski, Yale Joel/Time & Life Pictures, Kidwiler Collection/Diamond Images, Major League Baseball Photos/MLB, National Baseball Hall of Fame Library, National Baseball Hall of Fame Library/MLB Photos, Hy Peskin/Time & Life Pictures, Christian Petersen, Photo File, Tom Pidgeon/Allsport, George Silk/Time & Life Pictures, Ron Vesely/MLB Photos), Heritage Auctions, Library of Congress (Bain News Service/Bain Collection)

Library of Congress Cataloging-in-Publication Data
Names: Whiting, Jim, author.
Title: Cleveland Indians / Jim Whiting.
Series: Creative sports. Veterans.
Includes index.
Summary: Encompassing the extraordinary history of Major League Baseball's Cleveland Indians, this photo-laden narrative underscores significant players, team accomplishments, and noteworthy moments that will stand out in young sports fans' minds.
Identifiers: LCCN 2019060018 / ISBN 978-1-64026-301-7 (hardcover) / ISBN 978-1-62832-833-2 (pbk) / ISBN 978-1-64000-431-3 (eBook)
Subjects: LCSH: Cleveland Indians (Baseball team)—History—Juvenile literature. / Cleveland Indians (Baseball team)—Juvenile literature. / American League of Professional Baseball Clubs—History—Juvenile literature. / Major League Baseball (Organization)—History—Juvenile literature. / World Series (Baseball)—History—Juvenile literature. / Baseball—Ohio—History—Juvenile literature.
Classification: LCC GV875.C7 W55 2021 / DDC 796.357/640977132—dc23

First Edition HC 9 8 7 6 5 4 3 2 1
First Edition PBK 9 8 7 6 5 4 3 2 1

Infielder Al Rosen

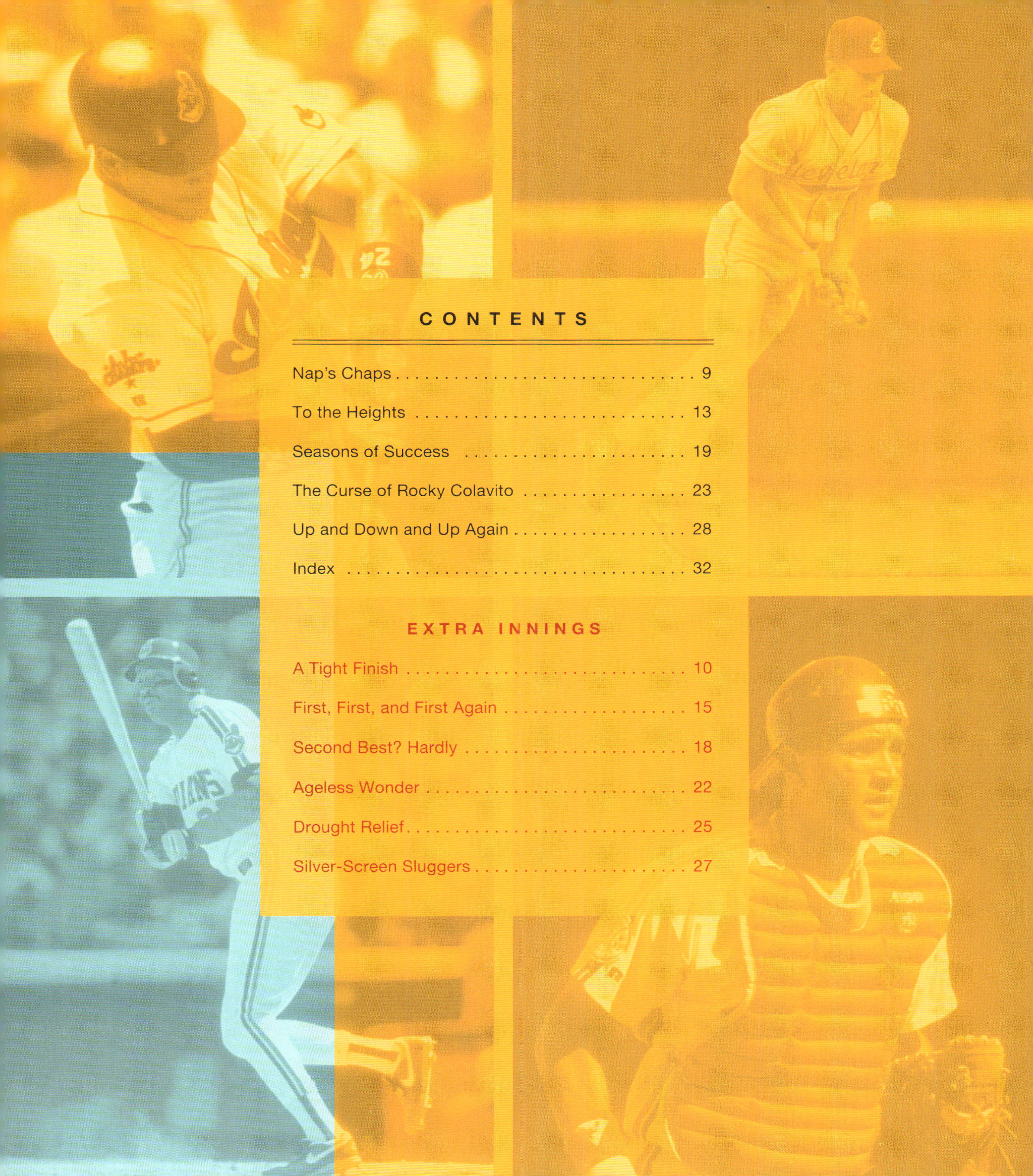

CONTENTS

EXTRA INNINGS

CLEVELAND

Second baseman Napoleon Lajoie

NAP'S CHAPS

Major League Baseball (MLB) teams have taken their names from many sources. Mammals such as tigers. Sea creatures such as marlins and devil rays. Birds such as orioles, cardinals, and blue jays. Some even take their name from heavenly beings (angels) and outer space (astros). But only one team has taken the name of a star player.

In 1901, eight teams formed the American League (AL). One franchise was located in Cleveland. Its players wore blue uniforms. Owners named the team Bluebirds, but it was better known as the "Blues." Players hated the name. It was changed to Broncos the following year. That did not stick, either. Cleveland struggled. It finished seventh and fifth in those two seasons.

In the meantime, second baseman Napoleon Lajoie had become baseball's first superstar. His career began in 1896 with the Philadelphia Phillies. Lajoie was a power hitter. Several times, he hit the ball so hard that the leather cover came off. In 1901, he joined the Philadelphia Athletics. He became the AL's first Triple Crown winner that season. He had a .426 batting average. That is still a record

EXTRA INNINGS

Nap Lajoie

Ty Cobb

A TIGHT FINISH

Ty Cobb of the Detroit Tigers and Nap Lajoie were neck and neck for the 1910 AL batting championship. The Chalmers Motor Company promised a car to the winner. It came down to the final game of the season. Cobb sat out. Cleveland faced the St. Louis Browns in a doubleheader. By and large, Cobb was disliked. Lajoie was admired. So the St. Louis third baseman played back on the outfield grass. Lajoie easily bunted his way on base seven times. The next day, some proclaimed Lajoie the winner. Others crowned Cobb. The *Sporting News* stated that Cobb's average was .384944. Lajoie's was given as .384084. Chalmers gave both players a car. It was eventually discovered that the totals had been calculated incorrectly. Lajoie was actually the champion.

for modern-era baseball. He smacked 14 homers and drove in 125 runs. He also led the majors in runs, hits, and doubles.

Lajoie left Philadelphia for Cleveland the following season. His new fans were not disappointed. He hit .379 for the Broncos. Sportswriters began calling the team the Napoleons, or Naps for short. "Nap" was Lajoie's nickname. The name became official before the 1903 season. Two years later, Lajoie took on the role of player/manager. The team was nicknamed "Nap's Chaps." The Naps had several good seasons under Lajoie's leadership. But they fell short of the AL pennant. Fans expected more. "He failed to lift up lesser players to the batting and fielding heights that he had attained so easily," a writer explained. "He knew how to do a thing, but to impart to another how it should be done eluded him." Lajoie's batting average also began to decline.

Lajoie resigned as manager during the 1909 season. He hit well over .300 for the next four years. But in 1914, Cleveland lost 102 games. One reporter referred to the team as the Napkins. "They fold up so easily," he said. Cleveland sold Lajoie back to the Athletics.

The team needed a new name. Local sportswriters suggested Indians. They thought the name was exciting. A newspaper cartoon showed an "Indian." He wore a headdress and buckskin clothing. He chased players from other teams across the field. Some sources claim there was also local tradition. Cleveland had a National League (NL) team in the late 1800s. It briefly had a sensational outfielder named Louis Sockalexis. He was the first American Indian in the league. So people sometimes referred to the team as the "Indians."

TO THE HEIGHTS

The name change did not help the team's performance. Before the 1916 season, the Indians traded for center fielder Tris Speaker. He played close to second base. He was almost like a fifth infielder. Yet he also chased down most deep shots. "Tris played the shallowest center field I've seen," said a sportswriter. "I seldom saw anyone hit the ball over his head."

Halfway through the 1919 season, Speaker became player/manager. The team finished second in the AL. Expectations were high going into 1920. Tragedy struck on August 16. Talented shortstop Ray Chapman was killed after taking a pitch to the head. Surprisingly, Cleveland rallied to win 24 of its last 32 games. It won its first AL pennant. Cleveland faced the Brooklyn Robins (who later became the Dodgers) in the World Series. The teams split the first four games. The Indians gave up just one run in the last three games. They captured their first world championship.

Pitcher Stan Coveleski

The rest of the 1920s featured fine efforts from such players as shortstop Joe Sewell. The 1921 and 1926 teams finished second in the AL.

Center fielder Tris Speaker

First baseman George Burns was named Most Valuable Player (MVP) in 1926. He hit .358 and stroked an MLB-record 64 doubles. But the Indians never seriously contended for the pennant.

On July 31, 1932, an overflow crowd welcomed the Indians to their new home. It was the 78,000-seat Cleveland Municipal Stadium. "When I went to the mound and looked around at the crowd, it was the most awesome thing I'd ever seen," recalled pitcher Mel Harder. "I mean, 80,000 fans. It was hard to believe so many people could be in one place." Unfortunately, the ballpark was not fan-friendly. Chilly winds swirled in from nearby Lake Erie. People soon called it the "Mistake by the Lake."

In 1936, fans had something to take their minds off the stadium woes. Cleveland signed 17-year-old pitcher Bob Feller. "Rapid Robert" lived up to his nickname. He had a sizzling fastball. It became the stuff of legend. Feller led the AL in strikeouts seven times. Chicago White Sox pitcher Ted Lyons could hardly believe the speed of Feller's heater. "It wasn't until you hit against him that you knew how fast he really was," Lyons remarked.

In 1940, Rapid Robert was hitting his peak. He threw a no-hitter on Opening Day. He won the pitching Triple Crown with 27 wins, a 2.61 earned-run average (ERA), and 261 strikeouts. The Indians played tug-of-war with the Detroit Tigers for the pennant all year. But they stumbled late in the season. They finished one game behind Detroit. Then the U.S. entered World War II. Many players, including Feller, went to serve in the military. The Indians put up losing records.

Bill Wambsganss

WORLD SERIES, GAME 5, CLEVELAND, OHIO, OCTOBER 10, 1920

FIRST, FIRST, AND FIRST AGAIN

The Indians established three World Series firsts. Outfielder Elmer Smith hit the first World Series grand slam. Then Jim Bagby became the first pitcher to notch a home run. In the fifth inning, Brooklyn's first two players hit singles. The next batter ripped a hard drive toward right-center. Both runners took off running. Second baseman Bill Wambsganss snagged the ball. He stepped on second base. Then he tagged the runner coming from first. It was the first—and thus far only—unassisted triple play in World Series history. "I've been in baseball 40 years," said Brooklyn manager Wilbert Robinson, "and I never saw one like this."

Pitcher Bob Feller

LARRY DOBY
CENTER FIELDER
INDIANS SEASONS: 1947–55, 1958
HEIGHT: 6-FOOT-1
WEIGHT: 180 POUNDS

SECOND BEST? HARDLY

Larry Doby was the second black baseball player in the major leagues. The first, Jackie Robinson, was elected to the Hall of Fame in his first year of eligibility. Despite similar statistics, Doby had to wait 39 years. Both played 10 seasons with their primary teams. (Doby played three additional years for other teams.) Doby was a seven-time All-Star. He hit .286, smacked 215 homers, and had 776 runs batted in (RBI) for Cleveland. "Jackie got all the publicity for putting up with it [racial slurs]. But it was the same thing I had to deal with," Doby said. "Nobody said, 'We're gonna be nice to the second black.'"

SEASONS OF SUCCESS

By 1946, Feller had returned. Still in top form, he won 26 games. He had a franchise-record 348 strikeouts. New owner Bill Veeck made sure that Feller was not the only attraction. Veeck gave out prizes to fans. He shot off fireworks. He drove relief pitchers to the mound in a red jeep. Cleveland finished sixth that season. But Veeck's attempts to make games more interesting worked. That year, attendance topped one million for the first time.

Veeck was also at the forefront of integrating the major leagues. In 1947, he signed center fielder Larry Doby. Doby became the AL's first black player. (Jackie Robinson had joined the NL's Brooklyn Dodgers the previous year.) Before Doby's first game, shortstop/manager Lou Boudreau introduced him to his new teammates. "All the guys put their hand out, all but three," Doby said. "As soon as he could, Bill Veeck got rid of those three." Veeck signed pitcher Satchel Paige in 1948. Paige had been a sensation for many years in the Negro Leagues.

Pitcher Bob Lemon had joined the team in 1946. Two years later, he led the majors with 10 shutouts. That helped the Indians tie the Boston Red Sox for the AL pennant. The teams met in a one-game playoff. Cleveland put rookie Gene Bearden on the mound. Bearden was lucky to be alive, much less pitching in a pro game. He served on the cruiser USS *Helena* during the war. A Japanese submarine sank his ship. Bearden suffered a fractured skull and a crushed kneecap. He spent nearly two years in a hospital. Now he was pitching in the most important game of his life. Bearden allowed just one earned run. Cleveland won, 8–3.

Infielder Bobby Avila

The Indians faced the Boston Braves in the World Series. Bearden continued his heroics. He won Game 3 with a five-hit shutout. He saved the series-clinching win in Game 6. "Gene Bearden, a carefree rookie with ice water in his veins, is the undisputed hero of Cleveland's first World Series triumph since 1920," wrote Jack Hand of the *Associated Press*. "'We owe it all to Bearden,' said manager Lou Boudreau."

Cleveland continued to play at a high level. It won at least 89 games for the next 5 seasons. But the team did not win the pennant. Then in 1954, Cleveland won an AL-record 111 games. Lemon and pitcher Early Wynn each notched 23 victories. Fans were confident they would win the World Series. Cleveland faced the New York Giants. Game 1 saw Giants center fielder Willie Mays save at least two runs with a sensational running catch in the eighth inning. The score was knotted 2–2 after nine innings. Then Giants pinch hitter Dusty Rhodes stroked a three-run walk-off home run. The Indians were stunned. They could not recover. New York swept the series. Cleveland fans hoped for another shot at the title. But the Indians fell just short of the pennant the next two seasons.

Shortstop Lou Boudreau

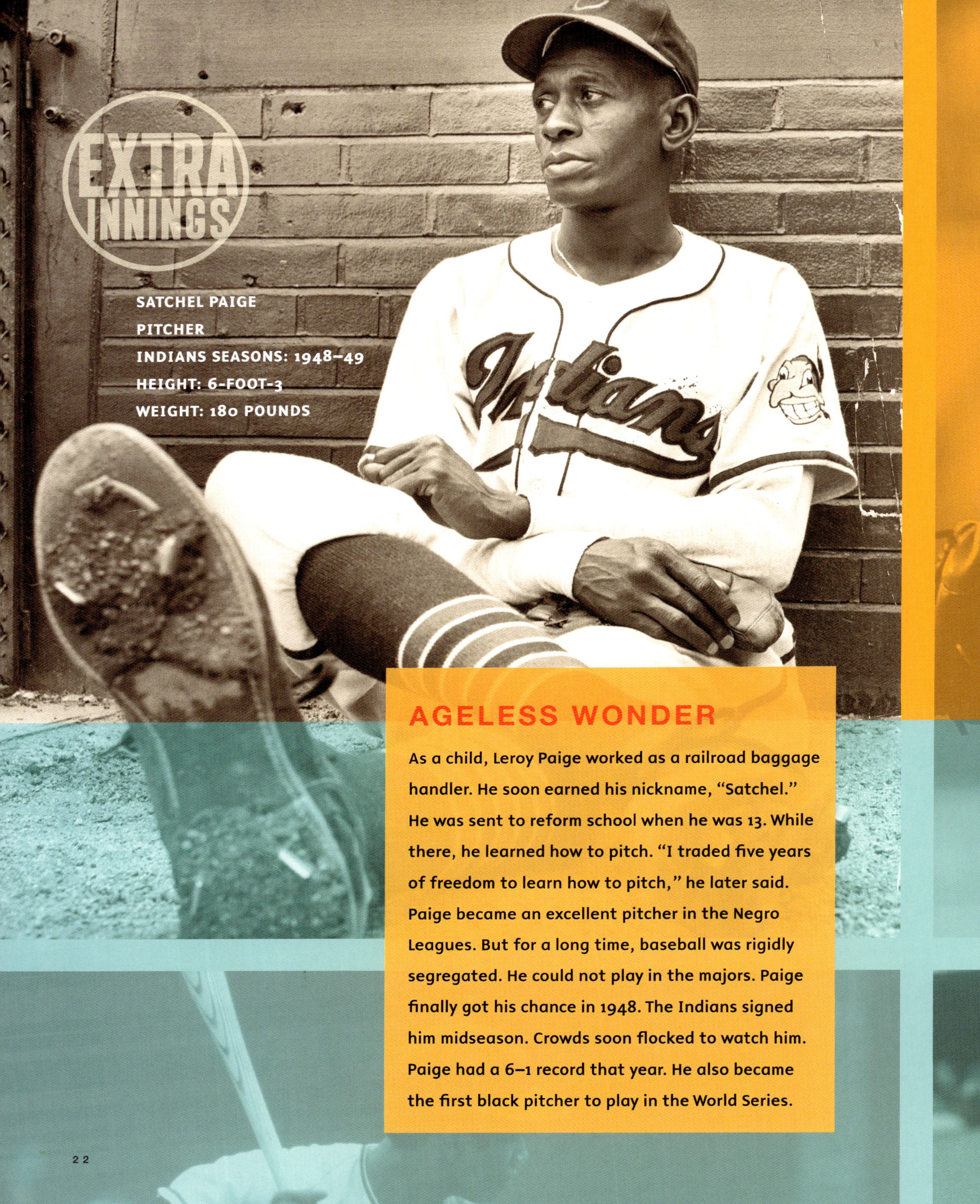

SATCHEL PAIGE
PITCHER
INDIANS SEASONS: 1948–49
HEIGHT: 6-FOOT-3
WEIGHT: 180 POUNDS

AGELESS WONDER

As a child, Leroy Paige worked as a railroad baggage handler. He soon earned his nickname, "Satchel." He was sent to reform school when he was 13. While there, he learned how to pitch. "I traded five years of freedom to learn how to pitch," he later said. Paige became an excellent pitcher in the Negro Leagues. But for a long time, baseball was rigidly segregated. He could not play in the majors. Paige finally got his chance in 1948. The Indians signed him midseason. Crowds soon flocked to watch him. Paige had a 6–1 record that year. He also became the first black pitcher to play in the World Series.

THE CURSE OF ROCKY COLAVITO

Professional baseball has had several infamous curses. One of the most well known was the "Curse of the Bambino." Babe Ruth had led the Red Sox to the World Series title in 1918. But Boston sold Ruth, nicknamed "Bambino," to the New York Yankees after the 1919 season. The Red Sox did not win another world championship for 86 years.

Cleveland's curse involved slugging right fielder Rocky Colavito. He joined the Indians in 1955. He belted more than 40 home runs in 1958 and 1959. He also had a powerful throwing arm. Colavito was a fan favorite. He stayed at the ballfield for long autograph sessions after each game.

Cleveland finished a close second in the AL in 1959. The 1960 season seemed full of promise. But general manager Frank Lane traded Colavito to the Tigers. Colavito was upset. "I loved Cleveland and the Indians," he said more than 50 years later. "I never wanted to leave." The Indians dropped to fourth.

The Indians received Harvey Kuenn in exchange. He was famous for hitting singles. "Last time I checked, a single doesn't count as much as a home run," a Cleveland sportswriter noted bitterly. Kuenn spent just one season as an Indian. The trade haunted the team. It failed to even qualify for the playoffs for 40 years. Fans called it the "Curse of Rocky Colavito."

Cleveland brought Colavito back in 1965. But his hitting steadily declined. One player the Indians traded to get Colavito back was pitcher Tommy John. John went on to win 286 games for other teams. That imbalance was typical of many Cleveland trades during this era. The team seemed to give away its best players, receiving little in return.

The league split into two divisions in 1969. Cleveland was in the AL East Division. Throughout the next 25 years, the Indians had just 4 winning seasons. In 1991, they lost a franchise-record 105 games.

Three years after that, the Indians moved to Jacobs Field (now Progressive Field). They also moved to the newly formed AL Central Division. The change of scenery inspired the players. The team started winning. In early August, the Indians trailed the White Sox by just one game. But a players' strike ended the season.

The strike carried over into 1995. The season started late. Teams played 144 games instead of the usual 162. Still, the Indians won 100 games. That was the best in the majors by 10 games. Six starting players had batting averages above .300. Big catcher Sandy Alomar Jr. and sure-gloved shortstop Omar Vizquel led Cleveland's defense. The Indians swept the Red Sox in the AL Division Series (ALDS). Then they beat the Seattle Mariners in the AL Championship Series (ALCS). After 41 years, the Indians were back in the World Series. They faced the Atlanta Braves. Atlanta's superior pitching prevailed. The Braves held the hot-hitting Indians to a .179 batting average. Atlanta took the title in six games.

The Indians stormed to an MLB-best 99 victories the following season. But the Baltimore Orioles eliminated them in the first round of the playoffs. Cleveland topped the AL Central again in 1997. It beat the Yankees and the Orioles in the playoffs. The team made its second World Series appearance in three years. It faced the Florida Marlins. The series came down to Game 7. It stretched into extra innings. Florida finally scored in the bottom of the 11th. Cleveland's hopes were crushed again.

DROUGHT RELIEF

One thing was certain about the 2016 World Series. One of the longest world championship droughts would end. The Cubs had not won the title since 1908. The Indians' last title came in 1948. Cleveland won three of the first four games. But it lost the next two. Game 7 was one of the most exciting in World Series history. It was tied 6–6 after nine innings. Then there was a rain delay. The Cubs scored twice in the top of the 10th. With two outs, Cleveland outfielder Rajai Davis drove in a run. But the Indians could not score again. Their drought continued. Currently, it is the longest drought among any professional sports team.

WELCOME TO C

EXTRA INNINGS

SILVER-SCREEN SLUGGERS

The 1989 movie *Major League* offered a fictional account of the Cleveland Indians. In the film, a money-hungry widow has inherited the team. She wants to move the team to Florida. She tries to drive fan support down by throwing together a roster full of losers and has-beens. Predictably yet comically, the misfits come together to find success. They save both the season and the franchise for Cleveland. The movie was a surprise hit. *New York Times* movie reviewer Caryn James wrote, "*Major League* trots out the standard formula but has the wit to make fun of it now and then."

UP AND DOWN AND UP AGAIN

The Indians captured the Central Division yet again in 1998. They topped the Red Sox in the ALDS. But they lost to the Yankees in the ALCS.

Power-hitting outfielder Manny Ramírez carried much of the offense in 1999. He set a team record with a whopping 165 RBI. "Manny does everything so effortlessly," said manager Mike Hargrove. "The ball just jumps off his bat." The Indians became just the third team to win five consecutive division titles. But the Red Sox topped them in the first round of the playoffs.

Ramírez left before the 2001 season. Strapping first baseman Jim Thome picked up the slack. The lefty clubbed 49 home runs. The Indians earned another trip to the postseason. This time, the Mariners sent them packing. In 2002, Cleveland fell below .500 for the first time in nine seasons. It had losing records in three of the next four years.

In 2007, the Indians returned to the top of the division. They mowed down the Yankees in the ALDS. Then Cleveland faced Boston in the ALCS. The Indians took a 3–1 lead. But they lost the next three games by a combined score of 30–5.

The 2008 Indians seemed primed for another World Series run. But injuries plagued some players. Others simply had disappointing seasons. Cleveland limped to an 81–81 finish. One bright spot was pitcher Cliff Lee. He won 22 games and lost just 3. He captured the Cy Young Award. The team compiled losing records for the next four years. In 2013, Terry Francona took over as manager. The Indians won 92 games. They missed the AL pennant by just one game. They slipped into the Wild

First baseman Jim Thome

150
Wilson

Infielder José Ramírez

Card game. Unfortunately, they lost to the Tampa Bay Rays. Still, Francona was named Manager of the Year.

Cleveland enjoyed winning records in 2014 and 2015. But it missed the post-season both years. It won the division title in 2016. This time there would be no early playoff exit. The Indians swept the Red Sox in the ALDS. They had little trouble defeating the Toronto Blue Jays in the ALCS. They met the Chicago Cubs in the World Series. Both teams had long world championship droughts. The series came down to Game 7. The Cubs pulled out an extra-inning thriller to take the title.

The Indians captured the division again in 2017. Their 102 wins led the AL. Pitchers Corey Kluber, Carlos Carrasco, and Trevor Bauer combined for 53 of those victories. Kluber won his second Cy Young Award. But the team lost to the Yankees in the ALDS. The Indians repeated as division champions in 2018. The Houston Astros swept them in the ALDS.

Cleveland continued its winning ways in 2019. With five games remaining in the schedule, the Indians were in a virtual dead heat with Tampa Bay and Oakland for the two Wild Card slots. But they lost all five games and missed cut on the playoffs.

Cleveland's rich baseball history goes back more than 140 years. Though the Indians have not hoisted a World Series trophy since 1948, fans refuse to give up hope. When Cleveland claims its next championship, the victory will be all the sweeter.

Pitcher Mike Clevinger

INDEX